My Very First Look at
Opposites

Christiane Gunzi

CHANHASSEN, MINNESOTA · LONDON

My Very First Look at
Opposites

CHANHASSEN, MINNESOTA • LONDON

www.two-canpublishing.com

Published by Two-Can Publishing,
18705 Lake Drive East, Chanhassen, MN 55317

Conceived, designed and edited by

Picthall & Gunzi Ltd

21A Widmore Road, Bromley, Kent BR1 1RW

Original concept: Chez Picthall
Editor: Margaret Hynes
Designer: Paul Calver
Photography: Steve Gorton
Additional photographs: Daniel Pangbourne
DTP: Tony Cutting, Ray Bryant

'Two-Can' is a trademark of Two-Can Publishing.
Two-Can Publishing is a division of Creative Publishing international, Inc.
18705 Lake Drive East, Chanhassen, MN 55317

ISBN 1–84301–081–X

2 4 6 8 10 9 7 5 3 1

A catalogue record for this book is available from the British Library.

Colour reproduction by Reed Digital.
Printed in Hong Kong.

big ball   small ball

Thick and thin

thick
candle

thin
candle

thick
brush

thin
brush

Can you see a thin paintbrush?

Full and empty

full box   empty box

Point to the pirate's hat!

Tall and short

tall
flower

short
flower

tall
building

short
building

What colour is the tallest flower?

Long and short

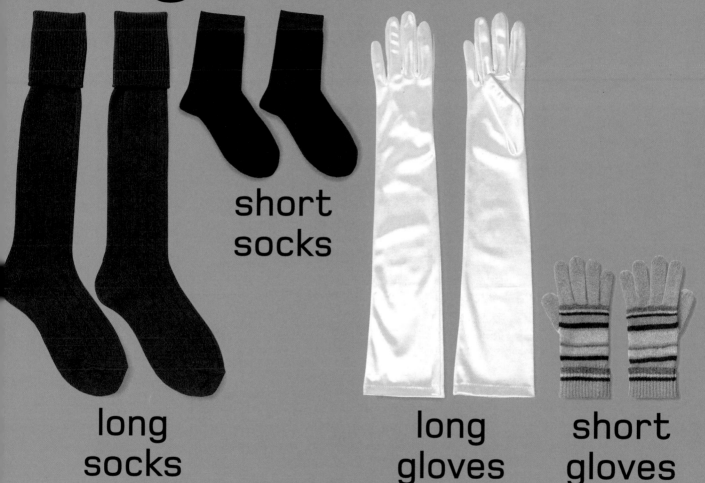

short socks

long socks

long gloves

short gloves

Point to the long gloves!

Front and back

teddy bear's front   teddy bear's back

What colour is the bear's bow?

n front and behind

the doll is in front   the doll is behind

What is the doll in front of?

Top and bottom

at the top

at the bottom

How many teddy bears are there?

Above and below

above the doll's head

below the doll's head

Is the blue balloon above the doll?

Up and down

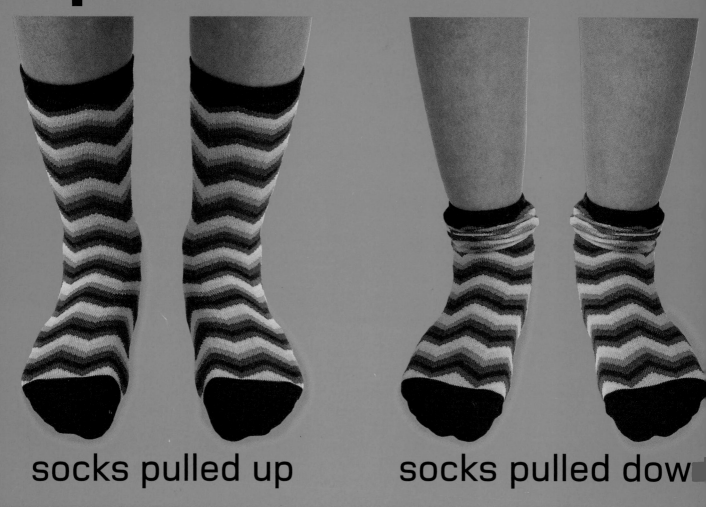

socks pulled up

socks pulled dow

Can you see the zigzag pattern?

Inside and outside

inside the box

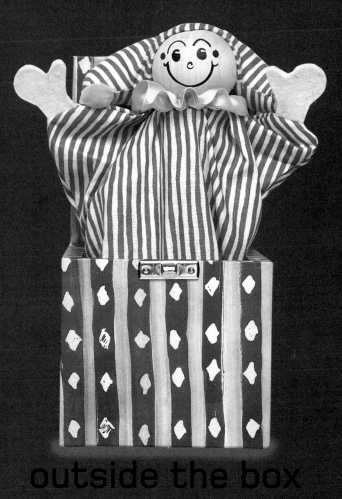

outside the box

What shape is the box?

Hard and soft

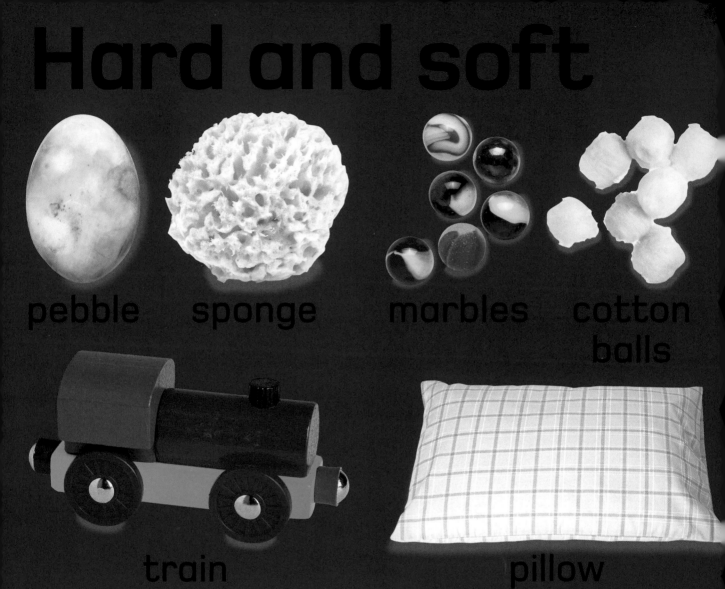

pebble sponge marbles cotton balls

train pillow

Which things are soft?

Clean and dirty

clean boots
dirty boots

Count the wellington boots!

Open and closed

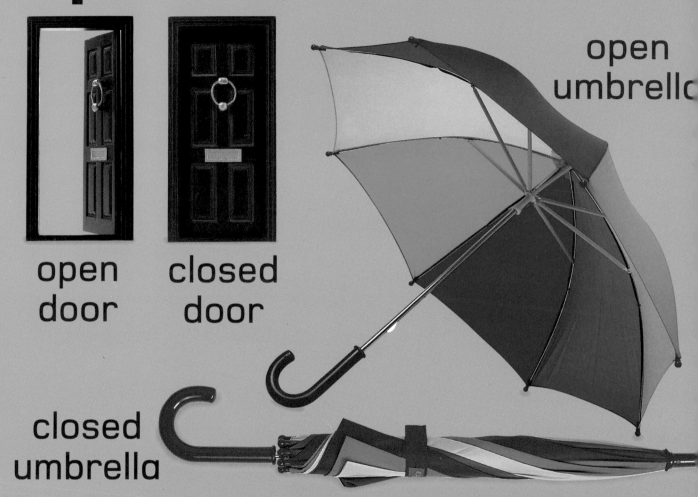

open door

closed door

open umbrella

closed umbrella

Point to the open door!

Left and right

left
hand

right
hand

Count the fingers and thumbs!

Black and white

milk

ink

coal

envelope

cat

cotton ball

Which of these things are black?

Day

daytime

Night

night-time

Point to the sun and the moon!

Match the opposites

top   dirty   front

clean   back   bottom

Can you find the opposite pairs?